THE OXFORD BOOK OF

Christmas Organ Music for Manuals

*including music for Advent,
Christmas, and Epiphany*

Compiled by
Robert Gower

MUSIC DEPARTMENT

OXFORD
UNIVERSITY PRESS

OXFORD

UNIVERSITY PRESS

Great Clarendon Street, Oxford OX2 6DP,
United Kingdom

Oxford University Press is a department of the University of Oxford.
It furthers the University's objective of excellence in research, scholarship,
and education by publishing worldwide. Oxford is a registered trade mark of
Oxford University Press in the UK and in certain other countries

First published 2017

ISBN 978–0–19–351767–7

Music and text origination by Katie Johnston
Printed in Great Britain on acid-free paper by
Caligraving Ltd, Thetford, Norfolk.

CONTENTS

INDEX OF CAROL AND HYMN TUNES

PREFACE

The pieces in this anthology of seasonal organ music for manuals cover the Church's year from Advent to Epiphany, providing attractive music for the listener, made approachable for players through the avoidance of formidable technical demands. Repertoire has been drawn from pieces written originally on three staves, here presented in arrangements just for the hands, as well as music conceived purely for manual performance. Transposition has been employed to enable use of less complex keys, while octave transpositions have been used as necessary in order to avoid wide stretches of the hands. Enterprising players should feel at liberty to explore judicious use of the pedal with the aim of enhancing the musical texture and giving additional strength to the bass line as is felt appropriate.

In choosing repertoire, I have sought to include as much stylistic contrast as possible, drawing music internationally from across the centuries. There are also commissions written especially for this volume. Such freedom in determining a contents list represents a privileged opportunity—work has been both exciting and educational through the fresh personal discoveries that I have made. I am greatly indebted to Frances Pond, librarian of the Royal College of Organists, for her unfailing patience and good humour in response to my innumerable requests for assistance in the course of three complete trawls through the College's unique, precious, and extensive resource. Her specialist knowledge has been quite indispensable.

Editorial policy has been to present a performing, as opposed to an urtext edition. Score markings have been kept to a minimum, with decisions on registration being left to the discretion of each individual performer. I am grateful to Jonathan Cunliffe of OUP for his scholarly advice and to Anna Williams for ensuring consistency in the presentation of material. This book would not have appeared without the enthusiasm of its commissioning editor Philip Croydon and the untiring encouragement of my long-suffering wife Pauline: this is a welcome opportunity to express personal thanks.

Robert Gower
Egleton, September 2017

Aria 'Bereite dich, Zion'

(Prepare thyself, Zion)

from the *Christmas Oratorio*

J. S. BACH (1685–1750)
arr. Robert Gower

Meditation on 'Veni, veni, Emmanuel'

('O come, O come, Emmanuel!')

15th-cent. French processional
arr. REBECCA GROOM TE VELDE (b. 1956)

Based on an anonymous 15th-century melody.

Chorale Prelude on
'Wachet auf, ruft uns die Stimme' (BWV Anh. 66)

('Wake, O wake! with tidings thrilling')

J. S. BACH (1685–1750)
arr. Robert Gower

Based on a melody by Philipp Nicolai (1556–1608).

Chorale Prelude on
'Wachet auf, ruft uns die Stimme'

('Wake, O wake! with tidings thrilling')

J. F. GREISS
(1720–68)

Energico

Based on a melody by Philipp Nicolai (1556–1608).

Prelude on 'Merton'

('Hark! a thrilling voice is sounding')

C. H. KITSON (1874–1944)
arr. Robert Gower

Based on a melody by William Henry Monk (1823–89).

Chorale Prelude on
'Nun komm, der Heiden Heiland'

(Now come, Saviour of the heathens)

ANDREAS KNELLER (1649–1724)
arr. Robert Gower

Based on a melody by Martin Luther (1483–1546).

Chorale Prelude on
'Nun komm, der Heiden Heiland'

(Now come, Saviour of the heathens)

KARL WOLFRUM (1856–1937)
arr. Robert Gower

Based on a melody by Martin Luther (1483–1546).

rit. al fine

Two Variations on 'Adeste, fideles'

('O come, all ye faithful')

THOMAS ADAMS (1785–1858)
arr. Robert Gower

Based on a melody attributed to John Francis Wade (1711–86). Presented here as performed on the Apollonicon in 1830.

con 8ve ad lib. al fine

Adeste, fideles (March of the Three Holy Kings)

from *Weihnachtsbaum*

FRANZ LISZT (1811–86)
arr. Robert Gower

Tempo di marcia moderato

Based on a melody attributed to John Francis Wade (1711–86).

Fughetta on 'Gottes Sohn ist kommen'

(God's Son is come)

J. S. BACH (1685–1750)
BWV 703

Based on a melody by Michael Weisse (*c*.1488–1534).

The Shepherds' Farewell

from *L'enfance du Christ*

HECTOR BERLIOZ (1803–69)
arr. Robert Gower

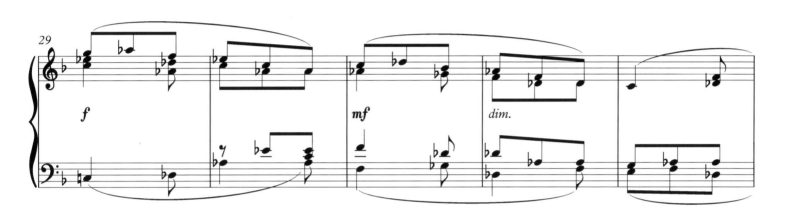

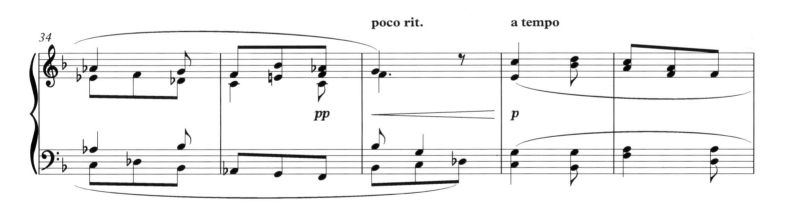

Joseph est bien marié

(Joseph has married well)

Noël suivi de 4 Variations from *Recueil de Noëls*

CLAUDE BALBASTRE
(1724–99)

+ signs indicate upper-note trills

Based on a traditional French melody.

Mes bonnes gens, attendez-moi
Majeur

For unto us a Child is born

from *Messiah*

G. F. HANDEL (1685–1759)
arr. Robert Gower

Weihnachtspastorale

'Vom Himmel hoch, da komm' ich her'
('From heaven above to earth I come')

ALBRECHT HÄNLEIN
(1840–1909)

Based on a melody by Martin Luther (1483–1546).

Study on 'Yorkshire'

('Christians awake! salute the happy morn')

C. C. PALMER (1871–1944)
arr. Robert Gower

Based on a melody by John Wainwright (1723–68).

How still we see thee lie

Prelude on 'Forest Green'

('O little town of Bethlehem')

OWAIN PARK
(b. 1993)

* signifies the melody

Based on a traditional English melody.

Jingle Bells

JAMES PIERPONT (1822–93)
arr. Alexander Hawkins (b. 1981)

for Roger Sayer

I Saw Three Ships in Sussex

MALCOLM RILEY
(b. 1960)

Based on two traditional English melodies.

for Paul and Heather Darragh

Toccata on Good King Wenceslas

MATTHEW OWENS
(b. 1971)

Composer's suggested registration:
bb. 1–8 and 135–137: 8' reed; bb. 9–87: Gt + Sw 8', 4', 2' (with mixture on repeat);
bb. 89–121: *p* Sw soft 8', *mp* flutes 8', 4'; bb. 122–148: Gt + Sw 8', 4', 2' mixture, and small reed.

* Optional use of pedal for chords on first beat of bb. 52–9 and in b. 148, where the chord may be sustained for an extra beat in a dry acoustic.

Whitehead, April 2014

Ding dong! merrily on high

Variations 1, 3, and 4

from *Trois Noëls en Variations*

GERMAIN RIVIÈRE
(1907–83)

Based on a traditional French melody.

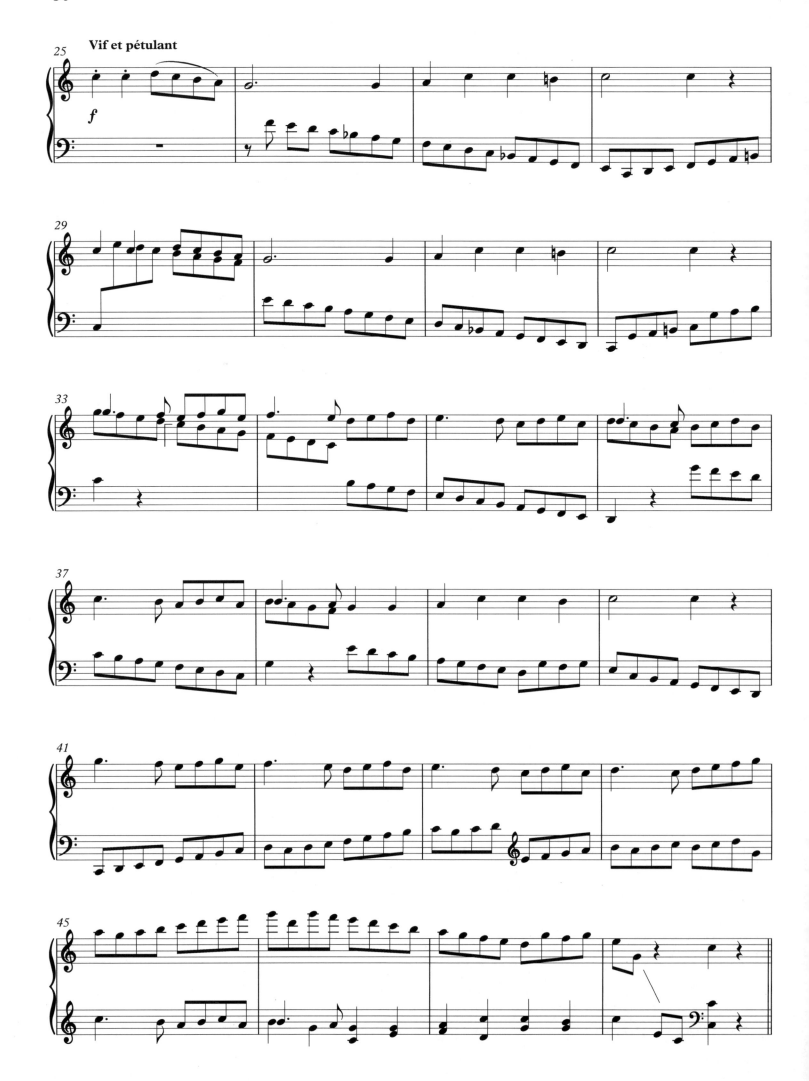

Verset on 'Quittez, pasteurs'

('O leave your sheep')

from *50 Noëls anciens*

LÉON ROQUES
(1839–1923)

Based on a traditional French melody.

Verset on 'Il est né, le divin Enfant'

('He is born, the divine Christ Child')

from *50 Noëls anciens*

LÉON ROQUES
(1839–1923)

Based on a traditional French melody.

Chorale Prelude on
'Vom Himmel hoch, da komm' ich her'

('From heaven above to earth I come')

F. W. ZACHOW
(1663–1712)

Based on a melody by Martin Luther (1483–1546).

Chorale Intermezzo on
'Vom Himmel hoch, da komm' ich her'

('From heaven above to earth I come')

JAN ZWART
(1877–1937)

Based on a melody by Martin Luther (1483–1546).

Pastorale II

from Suite *Kerstfeest* No. 2

JAN ZWART (1877–1937)
arr. Robert Gower

Chorale 'Vom Himmel hoch, da komm' ich her'

Stille Nacht

(Silent Night)

from Suite *Kerstfeest* No. 1

JAN ZWART (1877–1937)
arr. Robert Gower

Based on a melody by Franz Xaver Gruber (1787–1863).

Variation on 'Stuttgart'

from *Introduction, Variations, and Finale on 'Stuttgart'*

('Bethlehem, of noblest cities')

AMBROSE PORTER (1885–1971)
arr. Robert Gower

Based on a melody attributed to Christian Friedrich Witt (*c.*1660–1717).

rall.   a tempo   rall. al fine

Chorale Prelude on
'Wie schön leuchtet der Morgenstern'

('How brightly shines the Morning Star')

J. F. GREISS (1720–68)
arr. Robert Gower

Based on a melody by Philipp Nicolai (1556–1608).